WHAT IS SANCTIFYING GRACE?

WHAT IS SANCTIFYING GRACE?

LESLIE PARROTT

Beacon Hill Press of Kansas City
Kansas City, Missouri

Copyright 2003
by Beacon Hill Press of Kansas City

ISBN 083-412-0380

Printed in the
United States of America

Cover Design: Keith Alexander

Library of Congress Cataloging-in-Publication Data

Parrott, Leslie, 1922-
    What is sanctifying grace? / Leslie Parrott, Sr.
        p. cm.
Includes bibliographical references.
    ISBN 0-8341-2038-0 (pbk.)
    1. Sanctification—Christianity. 2. Perfection—Religious aspects—Church of the Nazarene. 3. Church of the Nazarene—Doctrines. I. Title.

BT766.P27 2003
234'.8—dc21

                                                            2003001474

10 9 8 7 6 5 4 3 2

This book is dedicated to
Stephen S. White
His degrees in higher education included a certifi-
cate from a small Bible school in Valonia,
Arkansas, an M.A. from Brown University, a Th.B.
from Drew Theological Seminary, and a Ph.D. in
philosophy from the University of Chicago. Dr.
White was in charge of the short-lived seminary de-
gree program at Olivet Nazarene College (now
University), canceled in cooperation with the
newly founded Nazarene Theological Seminary.
He was my favorite professor!

CONTENTS

An Introduction

The biggest battle during my religious pilgrimage was determining the validity of entire sanctification. I couldn't come to grips with it as the personal and spiritual experience that would do for me all that its advocates claimed. I embraced the theological concept of the new birth that was explained to me by my spiritual mentors. But entire sanctification as it was preached and taught was another matter.

As I look back on my years as a child and my young adulthood, it seems to me the Holiness preachers of that era confused human nature with carnal nature. The problem arose when they confused some of the (1) thoughts, (2) feelings, and (3) behavioral patterns that are God-given in human nature with the carnal nature. As a result, the altars were filled with sensitive people feeling guilty over their humanity. At first I was confused, and later I was just plain mad.

I wanted to be all God wanted me to be by His sanctifying grace. I sought it and sought it and sought it. I got it, and then I lost it. Then I started over again. But Dr. White brought me to the knowledge that sanctification isn't an "it" but a relationship. Sanctifying grace is the deepest kind of relationship with the Holy Spirit, the adorable third person of the Trinity. This relationship did not rob me of my individual uniqueness, my thoroughly human nature, nor did it demand of me a degree of perfection I could not achieve.

Dr. White—a professor who carried an unbelievable teaching load of theology, psychology, and philosophy in the same academic year—mentored me through my young adult years. All of these influences culminated in the experience described in the last chapter of this book. (This story is reduced and edited from the author's previous book *Renewing the Spirit of Revival*.)

Dr. White taught the first two courses I ever took in psychology. In Introduction to Psychology and Educational Psychology, he took the time to differentiate between human nature and carnal nature. This shed some intellectual daylight. He also introduced me to philosophy with Will Durant's *Mansions of Philosophy*. His textbook for theology, *The Christian Faith*, was written by his former professor at Drew Theological Seminary, Olin A. Curtis. Dr. White expected his students to digest that book, and most of us did.

My hope for the book you are now reading is that it will lead the way for humble, God-fearing believers to seek and find the sanctifying grace Christ provided on the Cross. Anything short of heart cleansing and the unconditional, empowering love of Christ administered by the Holy Spirit limits the power of the Cross. On the Cross Christ provided for the forgiveness of our sins, our state of justification before God, the regeneration of our nature, and the new birth by which we are made spiritually alive in Christ. *That is sanctifying grace!*

But on the same Cross, Christ also provided for the cleansing of our minds, the control of our wills, the discipline of our emotions, and the spiritual formation that molds our human spirits after the Spirit of our Lord. *That is sanctifying grace!*

Chapter 1 is an overview. The second and third chapters deal with the sanctification issues of "when" and "how." Chapters 2 and 3 are important in understanding the seeming contradiction between sanctification as **process** and entire sanctification as **instantaneous** experience. Chapter 4 is on "Wesley: Then and Now." As already suggested, the final chapter is the story of my own personal experience with sanctifying grace.

My prayer is that this book will increase your level of ease with the idea of sanctifying grace, that you will understand sanctification better, and that you will ultimately experience the joy of loving God with your whole mind and strength and that you will love your neighbor as you love yourself.

Leslie Parrott Sr.
Bourbonnais, Illinois
September 2001

1

WHAT IS SANCTIFYING GRACE?

"For this is the will of God, even your sanctification."
—From Paul to the believers in Thessalonica (1 Thess. 4:3)

Although I awakened as usual, I knew immediately that something unusual was going on! My sight was blurred; the scope of my vision was dramatically narrowed. Something was terribly wrong. Rubbing my eyes didn't help, nor did calling for help. My fear was becoming panic.

As it turned out, there had been an occlusion in an artery leading away from the retina of my right eye. At the doctor's office I got the bad news that I would need eye surgery. That pronouncement moved my emotional state from panic to long-term anxiety.

Due to sun-damaged skin, I was already a patient at the Northwestern Medical Faculty Foundation, so I asked the staff there for recommendations on the best eye surgeons in Chicago. They had no reason to know my church affiliation, so I was happily surprised to see the name of a Nazarene ophthalmologist on their short list. That information was reassuring. I didn't choose

him because we were members of the same church,
however. I put myself in his care because he had a supe-
rior reputation among his Chicago peers as an out-
standing eye surgeon—and he was also a Nazarene.

Eye surgery is done under a local anesthetic that
does little, if anything, to dull the mind or close the
ears. Although the doctor asked me not to talk, I
could hear everything clearly.

The operation was just under way when the surgical nurse said, "Doctor, who is our patient today?"

"This is Dr. Parrott. He's the president of our
Nazarene university down in Bourbonnais."

"I don't believe I know much about Nazarenes.
What do they believe?"

Responding to her question, the doctor began to
explain the meaning of sanctification to his surgical
nurse. I never heard anyone do it better. He was
straightforward; he did not use abstract theological
words. There was no Canaan language, nor did he re-
fer to any Greek or Hebrew word. He quoted no academic authorities. In his own everyday words, he related the story and meaning of sanctifying grace.

For me the time passed quickly. The procedure
ended, and he concluded his explanation of sanctification by saying, "I have a book by Dr. Parrott on
sanctification. In fact, it's on my desk, and I'll ask my
nurse to send it over to you."

Later in the recovery room, I affirmed the doctor
on the good job he had done explaining sanctification
to someone who seemingly had no previous understanding. My voice trailed off at the end with a plain-
tive, unanswered thought: "I wonder how many

laypersons could have offered that simple yet profound explanation of sanctification."

I could never write as fluently as he spoke. In these next pages, however, I would like to propose as well as answer several basic questions about sanctification:

- What does the term *sanctify* mean?
- When is a believer sanctified?
- How is a believer sanctified?
- What are the limitations of sanctification?
- What are the stages in the sanctification process?
- Who is John Wesley?
- How important is John Wesley's message today?

Before moving on to these basic questions, I would like to expand the scope of concern from laypersons to pastors and their staff. How many young preachers (pastors, clergy) could talk to a nonchurchgoing friend in casual conversation about sanctification and present it to him or her in a way that anticipated as well as answered his or her questions?

On two occasions, I have spoken at the Holiness Seminar sponsored by The Salvation Army for young officers who are struggling with their own quests for a more adequate understanding of sanctifying grace. Could it be that we need more help of this kind?

THREE KINDS OF DEFINITIONS

1. A General Dictionary Definition

Dictionary definitions come from scholarly wordsmiths who have gathered the standard vocabulary of a culture and then defined the meaning of each word. In *The Oxford English Dictionary*, the history of the word is included. In other dictionaries, it is not included or is greatly reduced.

I happen to love dictionaries. This fascination may explain the reason the faculty of an institution I once served gave me an unabridged dictionary on an impressive mahogany pedestal. It stands regally under the big clock against the wall in the entry area outside our bedroom, a place where it won't be disturbed. It's there every time I enter or leave the room.

Perhaps better proof of my fascination with the dictionary comes from a big comfortable recliner in our family room that my family lovingly calls "Dad's chair." That chair is unofficially reserved for me. Even nonfamily members tend to leave it alone. Recently, a high church official visiting in our home started to sit in it. I enjoyed watching the little vignette unfold. He walked toward the chair as if to sit down. Then he did a double take. His eyes took in the sight of the big chair and the tables on either side that were covered with my personal items—a dictionary, pencils, yellow pads of paper, books, and the like. I admired him as he turned away slowly to sit in another equally comfortable chair. There is something about that chair that makes it look like private property.

I often sit in my recliner to watch videos. It's a favorite nighttime diversion at our house. One of the things I enjoy about videos is my ability to control the process. With a handheld device I can stop the film without ever leaving my chair. I can reverse the film to catch a word that interests me. Then I use as much time as I need to look it up, think about it, or even write it down before I move on with the film.

I have never doubted the definition of a word in the dictionary. And I don't know anyone who does. We accept the dictionary explanation of any word in our language as the norm. Therefore, when I wanted the meaning of sanctification, it was as natural as watching TV to turn to my handy dictionary. And you can do the same!

A "Heartwarming" Distinction

When I located the word *sanctify* in my dictionary, I learned up front that it is a transitive verb, not an intransitive verb. I know that disclosure must warm your heart! But let me explain by falling back on some seventh grade English. A transitive verb is one that connotes action that changes something else. Therefore, to "drive," to "pound," and to "strike" are all transitive verbs. (1) Something, (2) or someone, (3) or some condition is changed by the act of driving, pounding, or striking.

An intransitive verb is one that evokes action or movement that does not change anything. Therefore, "to fly" is an intransitive verb because there is movement but the movement does not involve substantive change. Therefore, we have passed a mile-marker when we realize that a sanctified believer has been changed in both the process and the experience.

The Summary Definition

The dictionary further defines *sanctify* as a transitive verb that means "to make holy, to render sacred, to make spiritually pure or to cleanse from sin." It helps me to realize that this definition was not written by or for theologians, Bible teachers, preachers, or church officials. The definition comes from the work of etymologists whose business it is to say what words mean.

2. A Biblical Definition

A biblical definition of the verb to *sanctify* does not contradict the work of people who publish English dictionaries but rather enriches them.

The Old Testament Perspective

Oddly enough, the word *sanctification* does not appear in the Old Testament. The verb *to sanctify*, however, shows up frequently. It means to separate from the world and consecrate to or set apart for God. It may apply to people, places, or things. To sanctify anything or anyone declares that it or he or she belongs fully to God. A few of those things or persons sanctified in the Old Testament are as follows:

- The firstborn of Israel (Exod. 13:2)
- The Levites (Num. 3:12)
- The priests and the worship tent (Exod. 29:44)
- The altar (Exod. 29:36)
- The offering (Exod. 29:37)
- The Sabbath (Neh. 13:19-22)
- A man's house or his field (Lev. 27:14, 16)

To sanctify the Lord God meant to put Him into a category by himself as God, supreme and sovereign, with a rightful claim on His creation.

The New Testament Perspective

In the New Testament, *sanctify* was expanded to include the means by which believers are both separated from sin by the cleansing work of the Holy Spirit and filled with the love of Christ. When John 17:19 speaks of Christ as sanctifying himself, it means that He consecrated himself for His work as Redeemer.

Sanctifying grace is not only the means of separation to God from the world of sin but also the means for becoming morally holy. Now that we belong to Christ, we become conformed to His image.

- Eph. 4:1-3
- Col. 3:1-10
- 1 Thess. 5:9-10

A Twofold Provision

God has made a twofold provision for the sanctification of believers. (1) Sanctification begins when a person becomes a Christian, having received a new life in Christ implanted by the Holy Spirit. This is often called **initial sanctification.** (2) Sanctifying grace is also accompanied by the gift of the Spirit. It must be appropriated, however, through a moral surrender of our life to God. This is often referred to as **entire sanctification.**

This definition is explained most fully in Rom. 6—8. There is a time of spiritual crisis when self is dethroned in favor of an unreserved surrender to God and a life motivated by love for God and our neighbor. Sanctifying grace is also a continuing process that will never end until we are glorified with Him in the world to come.

3. A Theological Definition

A theological definition of the verb *to sanctify,*

while solidly based on Scripture, is enriched and enhanced by theological insight.

It sounds like an oversimplification, but it is not, when Dr. William Greathouse writes, "Singleness of intention is a definition of perfection."[1] I agree with him as long as the three key words—"singleness," "intention," and "perfection"—are also clearly understood.

A Disposition of the Mind

Again Dr. Greathouse states, when "God begins to write His law in our hearts and minds; this is the beginning of sanctification."[2] This results in "the disposition of the mind of Christ promised in Romans 8:1-11."[3]

Dr. Greathouse gives another clue to the meaning of sanctification when he says that "in entire sanctification we permit Christ who lives in us to become sovereign Lord of our existence. . . . Giving ourselves completely to God's sovereign claims on our lives, the Spirit fully indwells us, making Christ our sanctifying Lord. . . . The Christ who began to live in us at conversion, now reigns in us. In this sense, entire sanctification is the fulfillment of our conversion."[4]

I want to close this section on the theological definition of sanctification with another Greathouse quote: "To be fully sanctified is not to be a super-Christian, but to be a true Christian."[5]

A Definition to Live By

Dictionary, biblical, and theological definitions of sanctification may all be summarized in the words of John Wesley, from whom we derive our theological heritage: "In entire sanctification, the heart is cleansed from all sin and filled with the pure love of God and man."[6]

Paul and Sanctifying Grace

"And the very God of peace sanctify you wholly; and I pray God your whole spirit and soul and body be preserved blameless unto the coming of our Lord Jesus Christ" (1 Thess. 5:23).

Merely Justified

John Wesley spoke of believers who were saved from sin as merely justified. As yet they had not gone on into the fuller life of sanctifying grace. Wesley was not putting down the religious experience of the new birth but was relating it to the need for sanctifying grace. Wesley saw unsanctified believers as occupants who were standing in the doorway but had not yet entered the house.

"If we walk in the light, as he is in the light, we have fellowship one with another, and the blood of Jesus Christ his Son cleanseth us from all sin" (1 John 1:7).

The Song of the Heart

The walking Christian who is following the light of Christ sings:

Lord Jesus, I long to be perfectly whole;
I want Thee forever to live in my soul.
Break down every idol; cast out every foe.
Now wash me and I shall be whiter than snow.
—James Nicholson

But the regenerated Christian who neglects or refuses to walk in the holiness light that follows conversion should sing a parody on the old invitation prayer:

Lord Jesus, I long to be partially whole;
I want Thee part of the time to live in my soul.
Break down a few idols; cast out a few foes.
Now wash me a little, and I shall be some whiter
    than before.

The follower of Jesus who believes that Christ died for the forgiveness of sins but not for the full cleansing from sin limits the power of the Atonement. Christ came to destroy the works of the devil, and He did that once and for all on the Cross, where He sealed it forever with the power of His resurrection.

CONFUSING THE EVIDENCE

I sometimes think the most confusing problem faced by people trying to understand holiness is the variety of evidence—sometimes conflicting—that is expected to be visible in the life of a sanctified believer. For instance, some have claimed that the sanctified life is evidenced by an anger-free life. This is unreal. Many of the so-called evidences of sanctification are unreal.

I once heard a preacher try to make the point that a show of anger was proof of the presence of a carnal mind. He said, "I knew he wasn't sanctified because I saw the red rim around his collar grow crimson as it spread upward across his face." I related this story to a group of Black pastors in a ministerial gathering in the Republic of South Africa. When they thought about red in the neck and face as an evidence of carnality, they nearly broke up the meeting laughing. As one of them said, "We must have been born sanctified. No black man ever has a red face."

Confusing Symptoms with Disease

My brother is a cardiovascular surgeon. He once explained to me what happened to students in medical school when they concentrated too much on the symptoms instead of the disease.

"When we studied heart disease," he said, "a certain number in the class developed the customary symptoms, such as palpitations, rapid heartbeat, high blood pressure, or irregular heartbeat. The teachers always took those symptoms seriously. They'd call for a stretcher, and uniformed attendants would take the patient to the emergency room. The students left in the classroom would smile knowingly at each other because they knew their classmate wasn't ill. There was no heart disease present. That person had developed the symptoms because of the fear of getting the disease."

When they studied infectious diseases, there were always a few students who came down with low-grade fevers. I don't know what they did when they studied gynecology. But I do understand the connection between fear of a disease and the symptoms fear produces. At my age I am comforted by the fact that people who think they have Alzheimer's don't. The person who suffers from that dreaded nightmare typically has no awareness of his or her condition.

I've often thought this tendency to preach on symptoms was the pervasive theme of much of the preaching I heard while growing up. Human nature was often confused with carnal nature. Many an altar was filled with sensitive people who unwittingly went along with the ignorance that described human nature and confused it with the carnal nature. Some preachers promised an unrealistic personality change in a 15-minute sanctification experience on Monday night following a similar altar experience Sunday night for justification and regeneration. This confusion haunted me from childhood through early adulthood. I was born again and again and sanctified many times over—but not for long. When the symptoms of what I believed to be a carnal nature showed up again, my faith weakened, and I started over.

The Sex Drive, Et Cetera

Sanctification manifests itself in our daily struggles. For instance, the sex drive, which is part of being human, is God-given and intrinsically integrated into the workings of the human body. It is far too sensitive and complex to come from any source but God. It is neither carnal nor spiritual. But how these feelings of sexuality are dealt with and the behavior they generate can be disastrously carnal or gloriously spiritual. Along with the sex drive, God also provided the will to control it.

A sanctified heart helps us exercise our God-given will in sexual matters as well as with many natural human drives and emotions. For instance, there is a fine line between jealousy and competition, a hearty appetite and gluttony, or covetousness and motivation.

MY FINAL ANSWER

Sanctification is a spiritual process that begins with conversion and leads to an experience of entire sanctification following a full consecration and thorough submission of the self to God. This personal experience is then followed by a continuing, lifelong process of dealing spiritually with the human factors in personality.

2

WHEN ARE BELIEVERS SANCTIFIED?

"Have ye received the Holy Ghost since ye believed?"
—Paul's question to the Christians in Ephesus (Acts 19:2)

As far as I know, there is no denomination that believes there will be sin in heaven. However, this common ground does not eliminate opposing views on when believers are cleansed from their sin.

- Some believe in salvation and sanctification at the same time—that one is reborn and baptized in the same breath. But many persons have difficulty with the idea of being born again and dying to the carnal self in the same instant.
- There are others who believe one is born anew and then little by little grows into the experience of entire sanctification.
- Still others believe sanctification comes at the time of death. This concept confuses sanctification and glorification. Sanctification is both an experience as well as a process here on earth designed to bring believers into conformity with

the image of God. Glorification is the ultimate work of the Holy Spirit in perfecting saints for eternity. Death to the tyranny of self, not physical death, is the prelude to sanctifying grace for believers while they are still in this life.

WHAT ABOUT PURGATORY?

The chairman of the Department of Religion came to me one summer with a request from his faculty. "These 18-year-old freshmen arrive here each fall theologically illiterate. They are fresh from summer camps where most of them enjoyed an experience of warm, fuzzy feelings, generated around campfires in the evening and chapel services in the mornings. But they don't know anything about the theology of sanctifying grace. My faculty members voted unanimously to request that you speak on holiness during the first week of school." I agreed!

It should be mentioned that our university had a cohort of Catholic students who seemed to enjoy our Protestant atmosphere. For one thing, we had more in common with them theologically than with liberal Protestants. These French-Canadian Catholics believed in the deity of Jesus, the holiness of God, the depravity of man, heaven and hell, divine healing, loyalty to the church, and the work of the Holy Spirit. Besides that, we had standards of dress and behavior they supported. And they all attended chapel.

"NO SIN IN HEAVEN"

But on the Thursday morning I preached on "No Sin in Heaven," I wondered how the Catholic men and women in our student body would respond, since their personal salvation depends heavily on their relationship with the church, not on justification by faith and heart cleansing.

However, when chapel was over, I was quickly surrounded by a group of Catholic students who wanted to talk. When I asked them how they liked the sermon, one said, "We don't believe there will be any sin in heaven, either."

"Then when," I asked, "do you as Catholics go through the experience of heart cleansing?" Almost in chorus, they answered me with one word, "Purgatory." They explained to me why the funeral mass in the Catholic Church is so important. It is in purgatory that the soul of the departed is cleansed from all sin and prepared for heaven.

I don't tell this story to debate the purgatory issue, but to further illustrate the universal belief among denominations, and even other religions, that heaven is a sin-free society.

THE MCCLURKAN STORY

My mother and father came from Tennessee, where they were nurtured spiritually under the teaching and preaching of J. O. McClurkan. He was the founding president of Trevecca Nazarene College (now University), and his large tabernacle became the First Church of the Nazarene in Nashville. His spiritual shadow was substantial.

Dr. McClurkan believed sanctification was attained at the time of death. As a child growing up, I heard my father talk many times about Dr. McClurkan's sermons on this theme.

However, in due time, Mrs. McClurkan became deathly ill. She thought she was going to die. Dr. McClurkan thought she was going to die. Her physician held out no hope. At this point, Mrs. McClurkan reminded her husband that he had always believed a Christian could be sanctified at the time of death. Since she accepted her impending death, she asked her husband to call for some of the spiritual leaders from their tabernacle to come and join their prayers for her sanctification. The leaders came and prayed. Mrs. McClurkan was gloriously sanctified and attested the fact by a "spell" of "Methodist" shouting. But then another realization came over her. She had not prayed for healing, but she was healed! There was no more pain. The symptoms were gone. She felt well again. She was well!

After an interim to absorb all that had happened to her, she said (according to those who were there), "Daddy, what are we going to do? God has healed me and sanctified me all at the same time." Before she could go on, he interrupted her. "Honey, you keep the experience, and I'll go over to the study and change all my sermons."

MY FINAL ANSWER

- As I said early on in this chapter, as far as I know, there is no denomination that believes there will be sin in heaven. The question then is, When are believers cleansed from sin?

- My final answer is that the fullness of God's sanctifying grace is poured out on seeking believers who have consecrated their all to Him, have become submissive to His sovereign will, and received this sanctifying grace by faith.

A SUMMARY WORD

Sanctification is first a process that begins at the time of conversion. Attitudes and behavior patterns begin to conform to the new state of justification and regeneration. Then every believer, regardless of theological bias, in time begins to feel the need for a deeper spiritual work by the Holy Spirit. The religious crisis comes in a personal experience of consecration and submission, which is to entire sanctification what confession and repentance are to the new birth.

The spiritual crisis of entire sanctification results in a lifetime process of dealing with the shortfall in human nature that makes sinlessness and human perfection earthly impossibilities. This state of sinless perfection comes in heavenly glorification.

SANCTIFICATION IN SAMARIA AND EPHESUS

This secondness that characterizes entire sanctification gets significant help from two places in the spiritual narrative of the Early Church.

First, the Samaritan revival brought Peter and John to the scene, where they laid their hands on the new converts and prayed: "And they received the Holy Ghost" (Acts 8:17).

Second, Paul's visit to Ephesus is the occasion of

the second supporting passage recorded in Acts 19:2: "Have ye received the Holy Ghost since ye believed?" If your Bible says "when" you believed instead of "since" you believed, it does not really matter. The answer in both instances is no.

The secondness of the work of the Holy Spirit in these two passages supports the idea of the Holy Spirit coming on believers in a fullness or a presence not known in the new birth. When Peter and John in Samaria and Paul in Ephesus laid their hands on these believers and prayed for them, the Holy Spirit, who had entered them in the new birth, now became supreme in the fullness of His presence. Dr. William Greathouse describes this spiritual shift of power by saying, "In entire sanctification, we permit Christ who lives in us to become sovereign Lord of our existence."[1]

When the Holy Spirit was poured out on the Christians in Samaria, the spirit of revival spread to many other cities in the territory. When the Christians in Ephesus were filled with the Spirit, the greatest revival in the New Testament, outside the Day of Pentecost, began.

MY FINAL ANSWER

Entire sanctification is a work of God's grace wrought within the believer by faith subsequent to regeneration and is an ultimate personal experience of complete consecration and submission to the will of God.

3

HOW ARE
BELIEVERS
SANCTIFIED?

*"Present your bodies a living sacrifice . . . unto God,
which is your reasonable service."*
—Paul's admonition to the Christians in Rome (Rom. 12:1)

It is one thing to understand what sanctification is, another thing to understand when believers may be sanctified, and still another to understand how a believer may be sanctified entirely. Let's turn our attention to this third concern.

THE FIVE STAGES OF GRACE

The new birth does not happen in a vacuum. There are important stages of grace preceding justification and regeneration.

1. Prevenient Grace

Total moral depravity is the sinful state into which every member of the human race is born. Total depravity refers to the scope of depravity in the human race, not to its depth. There is a very important difference between total depravity and absolute depravity. "Total" means every facet of the human personality is infected by sin. "Absolute" means there is no redeeming quality that is even capable of responding to God. If man were absolutely depraved, he would live an animalistic existence. But in every depraved soul there is still the residue of God's grace, which is called prevenient grace.

Margaret Mead

Dr. Margaret Mead, the world-famous social scientist who did in-depth studies of the most primitive tribes and nations, particularly in the islands of the South Pacific, said she never found a tribe that did not have a concept of God and an order of right and wrong. That instinct for God and moral order is prevenient grace.

The Possibilities of Prevenient Grace

- Prevenient grace makes it possible for the most depraved person to feel the homeward tug of God on his or her soul.
- Prevenient grace makes it possible for the soul of an enslaved sinner to respond to the haunting truth in an old hymn or gospel song.
- Prevenient grace breaks up the dry ground of a hard heart and makes it possible for a sinner to be spiritually awakened or to feel conviction for sin.
- Conscience is first alive in every mortal because prevenient grace makes it possible.
- Prevenient grace is not saving grace. It is the grace that makes spiritual awareness possible. It

is the gateway to repentance and new birth in Christ.

In his letter to the Roman church, Paul said, "For whom he did foreknow, he also did predestinate to be conformed to the image of his Son, that he might be the firstborn among many brethren" (8:29).

God is not a passively angry tyrant who sits withdrawn and alone waiting for condemned sinners to seek out His forgiveness and His friendship. He is the loving Sovereign of the universe who is already seeking out the lost. The initial stages of that search are called prevenient grace.

2. Saving Grace

Stage 2 in the pathway to full salvation is the born-again experience known personally to millions of Christians worldwide and proclaimed in a plethora of songs, books, pamphlets, and articles. The story of Nicodemus in John 3 is a great supporting passage for this doctrine.

God's New Covenant

After lamenting how the children of Israel had broken their covenant with Jehovah (Jer. 31:31-32), God described the new covenant to come: "But this shall be the covenant that I will make. . . . I will put my law in their inward parts, and write it in their hearts; and will be their God, and they shall be my people. . . . They shall all know me, from the least of them unto the greatest . . . for I will forgive their iniquity, and I will remember their sin no more" (vv. 33-34).

The Three Promises

There are three promises in the new covenant underscored in the Scriptures and demonstrated in human experience.

First, there is forgiveness of sins through the blood of Jesus: "How much more shall the blood of Christ . . . purge your conscience from dead works to serve the living God?" (Heb. 9:14).

The Holy Spirit affirms this new beginning: "And because ye are sons, God hath sent forth the Spirit of his Son into your hearts, crying, Abba, Father. Wherefore, thou art no more a servant, but a son" (Gal. 4:6-7). "The Spirit itself beareth witness with our spirit, that we are the children of God" (Rom. 8:16).

God begins to write His law in our hearts and minds. We are not only forgiven but also changed. We are new people. Following a substantial list of character flaws that are not tolerated in the kingdom of God, Paul wrote to the Corinthians: "And such were some of you: but ye are washed, but ye are sanctified, but ye are justified in the name of the Lord Jesus, and by the Spirit of our God" (1 Cor. 6:11).

Sanctification in Process

Paul wrote the Romans about the relationship of the new birth to sanctification as process: "Likewise reckon ye also yourselves to be dead indeed unto sin, but alive unto God through Jesus Christ our Lord. Let not sin therefore reign in your mortal body, that ye should obey it in the lusts thereof. . . . But yield yourselves unto God, as those that are alive from the dead, and your members as instruments of righteousness unto God" (6:11-13).

Yielding ourselves to God for the purpose of changing spiritually harmful friendships, carnally motivated attitudes, sinful habits of behavior, and gaining control of formerly uncontrolled emotions is all part of the process of sanctifying grace following the new birth.

The sanctifying process leads all believers to recognize their need for a deeper work of grace. This leads the new Christian into the next stage of sanctifying grace, which is entered through the twin doorways of consecration and submission to the reign of God through the Holy Spirit.

3. The Grace of Entire Sanctification

Again, for help in understanding the royal road to entire sanctification, we turn to Paul's letters to the Romans and to the believers in Thessalonica: "I beseech you therefore, brethren, by the mercies of God, that ye present your bodies a living sacrifice, holy, acceptable unto God, which is your reasonable service. And be not conformed to this world: but be ye transformed by the renewing of your mind, that ye may prove what is that good, and acceptable, and perfect, will of God" (Rom. 12:1-2). "For this is the will of God, even your sanctification, that ye should abstain from fornication" (1 Thess. 4:3).

Observations on Rom. 12:1-2

The following observations on these passages may help clarify how a born-again Christian becomes sanctified entirely:

- Paul was writing to Christians who attended Christian churches. He called them "brethren, by the mercies of God."

- The major step in preparation for sanctifying grace is full consecration. "Present your bodies a living sacrifice, holy, acceptable unto God, which is your reasonable service." Consecration is to entire sanctification what repentance is to the new birth.

- "Be not conformed to this world: but be ye transformed by the renewing of your mind." In his translation, J. B. Phillips states, "Don't let the world around you squeeze you into its own mould." Separation from sin and sinful dispositions is an important factor in mirroring the image of God's love in our lives. This is why Paul said in another place in the same Roman letter, "Yield yourselves unto God, as those that are alive from the dead" (6:13).

Programming the Computer

The best analogy I know for what takes place in the transformation of the mind is the computer. It gives out what it takes in: "Garbage in, garbage out." Since the computer only responds as it is programmed, the only way to change what it gives out is by reprogramming. First comes the process of reprogramming the hard drive and then the instantaneous experience of pushing the button that puts the changes in operation.

The Christian seeking holiness (or entire sanctification or love perfected or the fullness of the Holy

Spirit) must open his or her mind to the transforming power of the Holy Spirit. The spiritual computer must be cleansed of the "garbage" of sin and reprogrammed to God's unconditional love.

A Filling Station Prayer

When I was young, one of my good friends and mentor was Jimmy Dobson, father of James Dobson of Focus on the Family. His early morning prayer sessions, straightforward speaking style, and obvious sincerity are still unforgettable. After a health break, he became a professional artist, specializing in scenes from the desert southwest. Eventually, he became head of the art department in a Christian university.

One day during one of our informal mentoring sessions, he told me the story of his striving and ultimate victory in entire sanctification, the experience he had prayed about for so long. It was during the depression days when the best job he could get was pumping gas in a service station. Small air hoses placed in strategic places where cars ran over them signaled him with a ringing sound when a motorist was in need of his assistance.

It was in this setting that he developed the habit of writing out his morning prayers. Almost every prayer was interrupted by the bell one or more times. But after tending to his customer, he would return inside to pick up on his uncompleted prayer.

As I remember Jimmy's account of his defining prayer for entire sanctification, he had been writing this epic life-changing "letter to God" through two or three customer interruptions. His was a prayer of consecration and submission. As he told me, he consecrated himself, his wife, Myrtle, his near-empty wallet, and everything else he could think of that needed to come under the sovereign submission to God's reign in his life.

Since it was his habit to begin each new segment of his "filling station prayers" by rereading what he had already written, Jimmy did so on this fateful Monday morning. At the end of his reading of the prayer out loud, down to the point where the ringing of the gong had interrupted him, the truth of what he had written hit him with force. Suddenly he realized that he had consecrated all there was to consecrate. He had submitted to God all there was to submit, including his very uncertain future. With a sound of triumph, he spoke and wrote at the same time: "Lord, I believe by faith this moment that You sanctify me completely from the top of my head to the tips of my toes." That prayer became Jimmy's spiritual North Star for the rest of his life.

Spiritual Insight Around a Tree Stump

During the second summer after receiving my degree in theology, I was invited to be the morning chapel speaker and evening evangelist for a youth camp held on beautiful grounds adjacent to the Hudson River about 100 miles north of New York City.

It was a great experience, partly because I got acquainted there with three young men about my age whose friendships I cherished throughout their lifetimes and now hold dear in my memory, since they are all in heaven. They were Homer Smith, Earl Lee,

and Ken Pearsall, all men who distinguished themselves in effective ministries.

After morning chapel each day, the four of us
gathered around a large tree stump just outside the
tabernacle where we talked theology earnestly as we
awaited the ringing of the bell for lunch.

Our favorite subject was sanctification, and our favorite theme was the list of unanswerable questions,
contradictory texts, and theologically gray areas relating to sanctifying grace. For instance:

- How could the thief on the cross have been sanctified as a second definite work of grace, since the
  words "To day shalt thou be with me in paradise"
  (Luke 23:43) indicated there was no lapsed time
  for the hunger of a deeper work to develop and
  the process of consecration to occur?
- We tested a key verse on holiness and found it
  wanting: "Follow peace with all men, and holiness, without which no man shall see the Lord"
  (Heb. 12:14). The time sequence was simply in-
  adequate for the thief to follow peace and to
  seek holiness, at least not in the way we had
  heard it preached. What about deathbed conver-
  sions? Just how long was long enough?
- Why didn't John Wesley give a clear testimony
  to sanctifying grace? None of us had done the re-
  search, but we believed that Gen. William
  Booth, who preached earnestly about sanctifying
  grace and replaced the Communion table with
  the holiness table in the places of worship, did
  not have a story of the sanctifying experience in
  any of his biographies.

- If sanctifying grace is the central goal for the be-lieving Christian, why aren't there more people who preach it, experience it, and testify to it?
- If a Christian has been cleansed from sin, how is it possible to ever sin again?
- Will there be any unsanctified Christians in heaven?
- Of all our discussions, none was more heated than the questions on sin. Is depravity the same as human nature? What about anger, jealousy, competition, and big egos, even in the lives of church leaders?

"Let the Spirit Do What Needs to Be Done"

One day while we were holding court on the sub-ject of sanctification, I noticed a pastor, Rev. Paul S. Hill from Long Island, watching us and listening to what we were saying. Pastor Hill had the reputation for being the nearest to sainthood of any pastor in the New York area. There was a transparency, almost translucence, in his face. His full head of white hair crowned his personality. He was truly a pastor beloved!

As he watched and listened, I hardly realized Pas-tor Hill was inconspicuously edging toward our group. Suddenly, without us realizing it, he was standing in our midst. Everyone grew silent as he began to speak. There was no scolding in the sound of his voice, no self-righteous tone, nor overtones of spiritual superior-ity. He spoke. We listened!

"I have been listening to you young men debate a lot of ideas and questions that, at best, are peripheral to sanctifying grace. I doubt if any of these issues is central to sanctifying grace in your life or the life of any other seeker. Just pray for the Holy Spirit to come in His fullness; and when He comes, He will do whatever needs to be done. You will not be required to explain it."

Just then the bell called us to lunch. As we turned quietly to walk away, I heard Earl Lee say, as though he were speaking to himself, "Saved by the bell."

From that day to this, I have never allowed an unanswered theological quandary to stand in the way of sanctifying grace. The prayer for myself and for you is: "I am ready, Holy Spirit, come in Your fullness! Do within me whatever needs to be done." When He, the Holy Spirit, comes in your life, you can count on it— He will do what needs to be done!

4. Maturing Grace

However, entire sanctification is not the end of the trail. In Dr. William Greathouse's book *Love Made Perfect*, he says that although the Spirit lives in us (Rom. 8:9), we are still living in a body with urges, drives, desires—though not sinful in themselves—must be put to death by the Spirit (Rom. 8:13, RSV). Like Paul, we must make our body our slave (1 Cor. 9:27).[1]

Paul leaves us with a number of reminders that in this world, we are not perfect. Although psychology, as a significant body of knowledge, did not enter academia for nearly two millennia, Paul fully understood the difference between the human personality and the biological self. In his letter to the Roman Christians, he wrote: "If the Spirit of him that raised up Jesus from the dead dwell in you, he . . . shall also quicken your mortal bodies by his Spirit that dwelleth in you. Therefore, brethren, we are debtors, not to the flesh, to live after the flesh. For if ye live after the flesh, ye shall die: but if ye through the Spirit do mortify the deeds of the body, ye shall live" (8:11-13).

Every drive that originates in our biological nature is not of itself evil. However, it must be kept under control by the power of the Spirit. This is the work to be done in maturing grace.

5. Heavenly Grace

Anyone who takes time to read the first six verses of Rev. 21 cannot but rejoice in the glory of the world to come. But even in the glory of heaven, the lives of the saints will not be passively static. We will serve Him more and more. We will continue to grow in His love. And for all of this and more, God will supply the grace. One of the great hymns on the bounty of God's grace, "He Giveth More Grace," was written by Annie Johnson Flint:

When we have exhausted our store of endurance,
    When our strength has failed ere the day is half done,
When we reach the end of our hoarded resources,
    Our Father's full giving is only begun.

His love has no limit; His grace has no measure;
    His pow'r has no boundary known unto men.
For out of His infinite riches in Jesus,
    He giveth, and giveth, and giveth again!*

4
WESLEY: THEN AND NOW

"And the very God of peace sanctify you wholly;
and I pray God your whole spirit and soul and body be preserved
blameless unto the coming of our Lord Jesus Christ.
Faithful is he that calleth you, who also will do it."
—1 Thess. 5:23-24

Somewhere in the alumni files of Oxford University is the name of John Wesley. He was England's 18th-century Billy Graham and much more. Historians say the religious revival he led in England saved that island from the kind of revolution that left France with blood in the streets.

WHO WAS WESLEY?

John Wesley (1703-91) was the 14th child of Samuel, a village pastor, and his wife, Susanna, a truly remarkable woman. She gave birth to 18 children and home-schooled them all, except those who died in infancy. She scheduled an uninterrupted hour each week with each child when he or she could talk about whatever was on his or her mind. Since the Anglican church her husband pastored did not have Sunday night services, she started meetings in her home that were attended by as many as 200 of her neighbors.

An Oxford Man

John attended Oxford University from 1720 to 1724. He left for a short pastoral experience and then returned in 1726 for graduate work. He developed a lifelong love for his university. When he was 78 years old, he wrote in his diary: "I love the very sight of Oxford." The room he slept in at Oxford continues to be rented to tuition-paying students.

Following a rotation system among the faculty, Wesley was invited in August of 1744 when he was 41 years of age to preach the annual sermon from the pulpit of St. Mary's, the university church.

Mr. Wesley, as he was called, would have been a strange sight to our eyes as he climbed the circular steps into the pulpit. He wore a long white wig, probably velvet breeches, slippers with large brass buckles, and a flounced shirt. He was short of stature.

But when Wesley announced his text, his voice, which was trained for outdoor preaching, filled the place: "And when they had prayed, the place was shaken where they were assembled together; and they were all filled with the Holy Ghost" (Acts 4:31).

Wesley's Impressive Legacy

John Wesley died in 1791 at 88 years of age, leaving a Methodist legacy that exists to this day. He left 79,000 Methodists in England, 40,000 in America, and a strong spiritual influence today on 40 million people worldwide.

But altogether as impressive as his numbers is the importance of John Wesley's theology of perfection.

What Is Christian Perfection?

The church Wesley grew up in was more of a political instrument than a spiritual force. A system of tax-supported parishes and pastoral appointments by a bishop whose term of office was for life left the church open for scandal, real and perceived.

The nation neither saw nor felt any indicators of the coming spiritual revival that would sweep the land, led by the two Wesley brothers from the small parish at Epworth. Few if any of the politically appointed clergy could have made any spiritual or intellectual contribution to the discussions on Christian perfection going on among Wesley's converts.

Wesley's quest for holiness began when he was 26 years old. While reading the New Testament in 1729, the Wesley brothers came to believe they could not be saved without holiness. From that point forward, John and Charles followed after holiness as they believed the Scriptures directed them to do and urged others to do the same.

Wesley's Favorite Holiness Scriptures

Wesley found the following verses helpful in his spiritual quest for Christian perfection:

- "Be ye therefore perfect, even as your Father which is in heaven is perfect" (Matt. 5:48).
- "Having therefore these promises, dearly beloved, let us cleanse ourselves from all filthi-

ness of the flesh and spirit, perfecting holiness in
the fear of God" (2 Cor. 7:1).

- "Let us therefore, as many as be perfect, be thus
  minded: and if in any thing ye be otherwise
  minded, God shall reveal even this unto you"
  (Phil. 3:15).

- "Therefore leaving the principles of the doctrine
  of Christ, let us go on unto perfection; not laying
  again the foundation of repentance from dead
  works, and of faith toward God" (Heb. 6:1).

- "For by one offering he hath perfected for ever
  them that are sanctified" (Heb. 10:14).

Aldersgate Was Not Enough

In May of 1738, Wesley joined a group meeting on
Aldersgate Street. While they were reading an introduction to Paul's Letter to the Romans, Wesley's heart
was "strangely warmed." This was a life-changing
event. But in time Aldersgate was not enough. The
scriptural goal of Christian perfection loomed larger
and larger on his spiritual horizon. As yet, he was an
unfilled believer who never lost sight of sanctifying
grace and perfect love.

Wesley's Plain Account

Wesley's 40-year spiritual pilgrimage—from his middle 20s to his middle 60s—was the gestation period for
his scriptural understanding and personal application of
Christian perfection. His definitive statement on sanctification was published in a little book called A *Plain
Account of Christian Perfection*. This booklet declared
his faith. This was his "Here I stand" statement that he

lived by for the remaining 25 years of his life. The following is my personal summary of Wesley's plain account. It was what he preached, taught, and lived.

The First Guideline: Christian perfection is attainable in this life. Wesley said, "There is such a thing as perfection, for it is mentioned again and again in the Scriptures." In the early stages Wesley focused on perfection, or sanctification, as a point in time, not a process. It was not until his more mature years that he fused the two.

Second Guideline: Christian perfection is a limited perfection. Wesley's limits of perfection were severe and clear-cut. Each limitation appealed to both common sense and human experience. "The perfect Christian," according to Wesley, "is robustly human."

- Not absolute perfection
- Not human infallibility
- Not technical perfection
- Not angelic perfection
- Not attitudinal perfection
- Not emotional perfection

Third Guideline: Christian perfection may or may not be sinless according to the definition of the term. Wesley said, "It is not worthwhile to contend for a term. It depends on the interpretation of the term." He believed that "nothing is strictly 'sin' but a voluntary transgression of a known law of God."

Fourth Guideline: Perfection is both instantaneous and gradual. Wesley believed that "a gradual growth in grace precedes entire sanctification, but the gift is instantaneous. . . . Sanctification begins with justification and continues after entire sanctification."

Fifth Guideline: The essence of Christian perfection is perfect love. Wesley believed that "sanctification is the process by which hindrances to man's effective love to God and to his neighbor are overcome. It is gradual, like the dawning of a new day." He also believed that the work of the Holy Spirit begins with prevenient grace. He found support for prevenient grace in the following scriptures: "But in every nation he that feareth him, and worketh righteousness, is accepted with him" (Acts 10:35). "Then Peter began to speak: 'I now realize how true it is that God does not show favoritism but accepts men from every nation who fear him and do what is right'" (vv. 34-35, NIV).

Guidelines for Today

Although John Wesley lived before the industrial revolution and has now been gone more than 200 years, his teachings are not necessarily outdated, as they have become in much of Methodism. I wonder what he would have done with "perfection" if he had lived after the Enlightenment or in our world of psychology, social sciences, and the advent of technology. In spite of certain concerns, here are eight facts I hold to, based on the sanctification theology of John Wesley.

First: Sanctification is clearly a Bible doctrine. I have attempted to demonstrate this throughout preceding chapters.

Second: We should use Wesleyan terminology, even though the terms may overlap: (1) sanctification, (2) entire sanctification, (3) Christian perfection, (4) perfect love, (5) holiness, (6) love perfected, (7) the outpouring of the Holy Spirit, and (8) the fullness of the Spirit.

Third: The filling of the Samaritans with the Holy Spirit. Acts 8:14-16 is a useful and excellent New Testament narrative on the subject.

Fourth: The New Testament Epistles provide the strongest scriptural support for the entire sanctification of the believers.

Fifth: There is a sanctifying process after the new birth.

Sixth: Consecration and submission are to entire sanctification what confession and repentance are to regeneration.

Seventh: The human will, which controls the human emotions, can be cleansed, but the glands are biological.

Eighth: Spiritual failure after entire sanctification comes in expected places. These include: (1) sexual purity, (2) human relationships, (3) obedience and service to God, (4) negative attitudes, and (5) the sins of omission. The possibility of spiritual failure will persist until the day we are glorified in heaven. "If we walk in the light, as he is in the light, we have fellowship one with another, and the blood of Jesus Christ his Son cleanseth us from all sin. . . . If we confess our sins, he is faithful and just to forgive us our sins, and to cleanse us from all unrighteousness" (1 John 1:7, 9).

5

THIS IS MY STORY

My life had every Christian advantage—or so it seemed. My childhood home was filled with stability and love. The first memory I have of my mother and father is in church. As far back as I can remember, I attended all services on Sundays and weekdays. And I was enthusiastic about attendance, especially the children's meetings.

CHILDREN'S CHURCH

I have always believed in separate services for children because of all I learned in children's church. Mrs. Rice was in charge, and she knew her stuff. Dramatic, illustrated sermons were brought by S. S. White, "Uncle" Charlie McConnell, and gifted people in the Bethany College community who knew how to communicate to children. We didn't have filmstrips, records, and videos of Bible events. We did learn, however, a solid set of biblical data that consisted of major passages for memorization. We learned the 23rd psalm, the Beatitudes, great Bible stories from the Old and New Testaments, the names of the books of the Bible, and how to find passages. General doctrine and basic principles of Christian living rounded out our "curriculum." When I went to college, I quickly discovered that my scope of Bible knowledge exceeded that of many of my classmates thanks to my children's church experience.

EGERMEIER'S BIBLE STORY BOOK

Another childhood advantage was a mother who took it upon herself to read me the entire *Egermeier's Bible Story Book*, a story a day. In addition to family prayers, there was attendance at every church event, even those sponsored by the district. Our church had great revival meetings, and all the famous Holiness evangelists ate dinner in our parsonage many times. As a child, they were my heroes and my friends. If it were possible for someone to achieve a satisfactory religious experience by absorbing the good atmosphere around him, it should have been me. All the theories about nurturing the Christian character should have worked if they were ever going to work. But somehow they didn't.

The secular theorists who claim that too much religion will turn children against it when they grow up would have predicted a violent reaction by me against the religion of Mom and Dad. I suffered from overexposure to church as some people do to too much sun. Then there were the restrictions. In many ways there was provocation for revolt. For instance, I couldn't attend high school football games, not because of my father's convictions, but because of the notions of some old ladies in the church who would have complicated my father's ministry if I had attended the games. I had to play my French horn in the high school orchestra instead of the band that I really wanted to join because the band not only played at athletic events but also presented an annual concert in an auditorium that was called The Theater. Many other restrictions like drinking soda pop from a bottle and not playing the card game of old maid followed this same distorted logic about shunning the appearance of evil.

No Prodigal but an Elder Brother

My hang-ups were not those of the prodigal son but those of the self-righteous brother, the good guy who stayed home and behaved himself. I was never tempted to revolt. I didn't even slip off to the movies when nearly every other church teenager I knew did. I lived comfortably within the limits of the written, as well as the unwritten, law of both the church and the home.

Dante was right when he put the sins of the spirit in the hottest regions of hell. There is no fire that burns hotter on the inside of a man than the flames of self-righteousness and self-pity.

In one word, my problem was people. There was the "lovable old gentleman" in our church who came to the parsonage and spoke disrespectfully to my father; the Sunday School teacher who called me a "smart aleck" when I asked him for the dime he promised us for each new boy we brought; the camp meeting president who put me down over something I couldn't help or change. In later years, a series of unfortunate events contrived to fuel my fires of resentment, which finally blazed into the white heat of bitterness. I became a cynic. In my outward goodness I chose to be hurt easily and then responded with a blazing self-righteous judgment that surfaced in fault-finding and self-pity.

At one point I became a specialist in the foibles of the church. The General and Special Rules, the doctrinal statement, the organizational and governmental procedures that had been hammered out on the anvils of Scripture, human experience, corporate conscience, and logic were the objects of my scorn. The theological alternatives of liberalism and Calvinism were explored with intense interest. But I found the lack of authority in liberal Protestantism and the rational legalism of Calvinism less perfect than the experience-centered theology of my own church.

It would seem that these academic forays into alternative theologies would have had a settling effect, but they didn't. Intellectual light did not illuminate the darkness of my spirit. Frustrated by the people I let hurt me and the church I could not really dismiss, the next step toward my spiritual dead end was self-hate, which became enormous simply by turning all my frustrated energies inward against myself. Jealousy, resentment, and self-pity flourished as never before.

THE UGLY SYMPTOMS

The symptoms were easily recognizable: My feelings were too easily hurt. I was destroyed inwardly by my contradictory feelings of inadequacy and the show of a phony self-confidence I developed as a compensating factor. Other people's successes—especially those with whom I compared myself—fired the blaze of smoldering confusion and misunderstanding within me. I told people off if I thought the risk of their retaliation was low. I gave every conversation a critical turn. Hurt invited hurt, like the magnet that draws the slivers of steel. Tears of pure anguish flowed out of a dead-end desperation.

A LIFE TRANSFORMED!

But on a Monday night in Salem, Oregon, by the side of the bed in the low-rent, second-floor apartment where Lora Lee and I lived while I was enrolled in graduate school, something wonderful happened. We had attended a revival service earlier in the evening. The evangelist, Bill Fisher, was an excellent preacher, and the pastor, Orville Jenkins, was a great person (later elected general superintendent). But they were not the agents of my salvation.

During this service, as we sat near the front on the right side next to the wall, I came to the end of myself. All at once I came to see myself as I really was—self-centered, bitter, faultfinding, hurt, jealous, full of self-pity. All at once I realized that my problem was not people, but me, not somebody out there, but me on the inside. I was at the end of myself, and I knew it. The only hope for me was a whole new beginning with a new set of motives and attitudes that could change my way of thinking about people and about myself.

It was during this service that something else came to me with full force. Sanctification and a life dominated by the Holy Spirit are basic New Testament truths. It did not matter from then on if anyone or everyone was a hypocrite and nobody really practiced the ideals of the sanctified life. Somehow I knew the fullness of the Spirit was about to transform my life. And no one needed it more than I did.

I suppose I would have gone to a public altar if an invitation had been given, but none was. Maybe it was just as well, for this was a very personal, traumatic experience. Back in the apartment, the two of us—Lora Lee and I—knelt by the side of the bed with my Bible open before us. I was so miserable I never even thought to pray for her. Theology was not my concern as I told God how miserable I was—as if He didn't know! I confessed all the miserable habits of thinking I had developed and nurtured. I asked forgiveness for all the ways I had put down my detractors. I told God I believed in the truth of New Testament holiness whether or not anyone ever consistently lived the life.

Putting all the people I knew on the altar, never to judge them again, was a gigantic step. Finally, I told the Lord I knew His Spirit could clean up all that needed to be cleaned up—complete cleansing had been a real theological hang-up for me—and the full presence of the Holy Spirit could renew my mind and take over my life. Without any real begging or pleading I just waited for Him to come. And He did.

I have heard other people talk about great feelings that overwhelmed them when they were sanctified, but I didn't really experience anything like that. Mostly, I just had a deep abiding feeling that from now on everything was going to be different. And it has been different. So different that I seldom go to Salem, Oregon, without taking time to drive by the apartment where my life in Him really began.

LIFE HAS NOT CHANGED THAT MUCH

The external factors in life haven't been that different. Life still has its bumps, its low spots, inequities, and inconsistencies. But from then until now I have lived a different kind of life. Sometimes it seems I live a charmed life. I wouldn't go back to the other kinds of attitudes for anything in the world. Things still happen that complicate my existence. But when they do, it is wonderful to see how God works it out. Each stage of life has its own unique challenges and problems. But since the day I died to a carnal, self-centered, resentful way of life those many years ago, my new life in Christ has never been tarnished by a lapse of His abiding presence. The problems I create myself and the ones others create for me and the ones created for me by circumstances are all in His care.

A LIFELONG JOURNEY

Through the years I've come to learn that this sanctified life is more than the experience of an instant. It is also a pilgrimage, a way of life. It began in Salem (Lora Lee was sanctified about 10 days later), but it has taken me from coast to coast, from the Northwest to New England and the Midwest, through the raising of three sons, and the infinite variety of frustrations, inner conflicts, and pressures that the stress of life gives each of us. This new life began in a revival, but it has continued through a daily renewal.

For me to reduce to prescription what happened to me through the renewing of the Spirit would be a contradiction of the process. An oversimplified analysis, complete with neat categories, results in what has been called the tyranny of the formula. There is a tailor-made quality about the renewal of the inner self that is unique to the work of the Holy Spirit. Reductionism is the peril of those who philosophize. However, since the Holy Spirit brought a thorough rejuvenation of my attitudes and my life beginning with the deeply moving experience I had in Salem, I have noticed several directions within me, led by my spirit, that are fed by living springs—in fact, the Source.

1. *It continues to become easier and less threatening for me to accept personal responsibility for my problems instead of blaming others.* For most of my life, living had been a matter of muddling through. Instead of using the knowledge and resources of God that were at my disposal, I was trying to navigate life on my own, making many costly and needless mistakes and wasting much of my potential for achieving what God wanted me to do.

Behind the brave front of confidence lay deep-seated feelings of bewilderment, inadequacy, and unhappiness. The price for muddling through is a high one. At the very least, it had led to an incredible and unnecessary waste of my inner resources. And at its worst, it had taken a high toll in unnecessary failures, lost satisfactions, and emotional wear and tear. One of the most frustrating games I played on so many occasions was that of lost satisfaction: "What might have been."

Prior to sanctifying grace, I thought I could manage under my own steam. After all, I was attending graduate school and paying my own way. Lora Lee owned three candy businesses. But the mistakes of ignorance and immaturity have a way of catching up with us. Violations of the laws of God in human nature are inevitably punished.

As the psychologist Herrick says, "Transgression of these laws brings its own penalty. No prosecutor is required. If you drink whiskey to excess, your health is impaired. If you drink wood alcohol, you die. . . . The wages of sin is death if not of the person, certainly of his richest values and satisfactions. And ignorance of the law excuses no man."[1]

It is a sad but unarguable fact that most human beings go through their lives only partially aware of the full range of their potential. This is good self-renewal doctrine. The person who has become a stranger to himself or herself has lost the capacity for a continuing life of renewal in the Spirit. By performing instead of living, a person becomes separated from the wellsprings of his or her own being where the fullness of the Spirit meets the need of the moment.

2. *Another developing area in my pilgrimage with Christ has been death to the fear of failure.* I cannot win all the time—nor should I. Before the Holy Spirit indwelt my life, I had to win or I simply did not play the game. At least I needed a good, solid rationale for failing to win that placed the responsibility on somebody else's failure rather than my own. This is what Mertin R. Rice called "the courage of imperfections."[2] The Holy Spirit has helped me recognize the great amount of human weakness there is in my nature. But He also helps me keep on learning when learning is risky business. Although growth cannot help but result in ad-

justment pains, the Lord is still helping me learn how to take my work seriously—but not myself.

When the child is learning at a truly phenomenal rate, a rate never to be achieved in adult life, he or she is also experiencing a shattering number of failures. Watch a small child you know, and see the innumerable times he or she tries and fails. But also see how little the failures discourage the child. Maybe this is what Jesus had in mind for me when He said that unless we become as little children, we cannot enter the kingdom of heaven.

Even to write this book, the very first line of it, called on my resources of courage. There is the distinct possibility of failing to write down the very lines that would help the people I hope to reach. One of the virtues of a high school and college education is that the formal process of learning requires a student to test himself or herself in a great variety of activities that are not of his or her own choosing. Again and again God has exposed me to special courses in the school of prayer, seminars in the college of faith, and even postgraduate courses in how to create faith where there is none.

I used to pay a heavy price for fear of failure. I know it was a powerful obstacle to my spiritual growth. In all of us, this fear assures the progressive narrowing of the personality and prevents exploration and experimentation. I even came to the place many years ago when I put the entire hierarchy of the church on the altar. Oh, what a relief! When I lost my fear of authority figures, I really began to love and appreciate them.

If you carry the ball, you can also fumble it. If you lead the band, you will face the music. But if you and I want to keep on learning how to walk with Him, we must allow the Spirit to develop within us the courage of imperfection. We need to get away from the "paralysis of analysis." When Max Planck was awarded the Nobel prize, he said that looking back over the long path that had led to his discovery of the quantum theory had vividly reminded him of Goethe's saying, "Men will always be making mistakes as long as they are striving after something."

3. *The Spirit is still teaching me to accept people the way they are instead of the way I wish they were.* On my pilgrimage since the zero hour in Salem, the Holy Spirit has helped me develop mutually fruitful relationships with an increasing number of human beings. I cannot be friends with everybody. But in an increasing number of instances, the Holy Spirit has helped me learn the ways of developing openness that allows the integrity of genuine friendship to develop.

Before the Holy Spirit came in His fullness into my life, this could never have happened. I liked people who had the same prejudices I had. I could not really respect anybody who did not come up to my standards of perfection. Since I was very defensive about my own role and status in every situation, I was easily hurt. And once hurt, I did not soon forget.

The Holy Spirit has helped me learn that, starting with myself, I am dealing with partial people. He has helped me learn how to accept people as they are at the moment. I'll have to wait for them to blossom.

The Holy Spirit constantly teaches me more and

more how to expect love and how to give it—both more difficult achievements than I used to think. He is making it easier for me to depend on others and not feel that others are putting me down. And I am learning how to be depended on without feeling proud.

Through the spirit of renewal I am continuing to learn to see life through another's eyes and feel it through another's heart. This is as it must be in the sanctified life. The man or woman who cannot achieve these relationships is imprisoned, cut off from a great part of the world of life. The Holy Spirit helps us see that the joy and suffering of those we love is part of our own personal experience. Love and friendship dissolve the rigidities of the isolated self, force new perspectives, alter judgments, and keep in working order the emotional force on which human relationships must function.

4. *Finally, it seems to me the Holy Spirit has cleansed my motivations.* John W. Gardner says, "The walls which hem a man in as he grows older form channels of least resistance. If he stays in the channels, all is easy. To get out requires some extra drive, enthusiasm, or energy."[3]

Before the Spirit took up His full abode in my life, I did not lack for motivation. The basic human drive for survival expressed itself in me in a spirit of competition that made winning the only thing. In churches where Lora Lee and I held revivals in those early days, we put on Sunday School rallies that broke all records. We even carried a supply of old vinyl records that could be displayed and physically broken on the morning of the Sunday School rally. Looking back, I wonder what proportion of our satisfaction came from exceeding every previous record and what proportion came from reaching new people with the gospel.

I have taught college courses on motivation and believe I understand the theoretical dynamics of motivation and emotion. I know that to some degree, motivation is a matter of sheer physical energy and high metabolism. No matter how intellectual or spiritual one's interest may be, there is an immensely important physical element in the capacity to learn, grow, recover from defeats, surmount obstacles, and live life with vitality and resilience. But none of this makes it necessary to grind your neighbor into the dust.

First of all, I think the Holy Spirit helps us learn how to lose graciously. Further, He teaches us the important lesson of learning to compete with our best selves. Measuring our own achievements by how far we have come is much more important in the Spirit-filled life than excelling over our neighbor who may have started the race from a different set of starting blocks.

Any student of motivation knows there are astonishing sources of energy that seem to be available to those who enjoy what they are doing or find special meaning in their lives. There is no one for whom this is more true than the man or woman who lives in the Spirit. Total commitment generates energy from sources otherwise untapped. Sorting out the difference between what is my problem and what is somebody else's problem reduces the need for extraordinary amounts of energy. Placing insoluble problems into the hands of God and leaving them frees the mind free for creativity and gives the body a chance to restore itself. I do not claim to have learned all these lessons perfectly; I am still growing and still on my pilgrimage with Him. But as I look back and then look ahead, it seems to me the Holy Spirit has moved significantly in my life in the adjustment of my sources of motivation.

What happens to the Christian who has lost his motivation is tragic. Ralph Waldo Emerson said, "Once we had wooden chalices and golden priests; now we have golden chalices and wooden priests."[4] Although he was no theologian, Emerson was saying something fundamental about the relationships of men to their institutions. It is easier to reorganize the church than to renew the spirit of the church. The church has been created out of ardor and conviction fueled by the fires of the Holy Spirit. As its assets expand, it is easy for its ardor to wane. As the buildings grow bigger and better, there must be the motivations that keep the spirit from thinning out. Nothing is more readily observable in the life of church organizations than the triumphs of form over spirit. Great ventures often start with vision and end with a power structure. The only antidote to this tragedy in your life and mine and in the church we love is a continual renewal of the spirit.

Notes

Chapter 1

1. William M. Greathouse, *Love Made Perfect: Foundations for the Holy Life* (Kansas City: Beacon Hill Press of Kansas City, 1997), 38.

2. Ibid., 48.

3. Ibid.

4. Ibid., 59.

5. Leslie Parrott, *Fulfilled Life* (Kansas City: Nazarene Publishing House, 1976), 17.

6. John Wesley, *The Works of John Wesley*, ed. Thomas Jackson, 3rd ed., 14 vols. (London: Methodist Book Room, 1872; reprint, Kansas City: Beacon Hill Press of Kansas City, 1978), 5: 23.

Chapter 2

1. Greathouse, *Love Made Perfect*.

Chapter 3

1. Greathouse, *Love Made Perfect*, 59.

Chapter 5

1. Herrick, lecture heard by author at the University of Illinois, 1949.

2. Mertin R. Rice, quoted by author from an unpublished sermon, n.d.

3. John W. Gardner, *Self-Renewal: The Individual and the Innovative Society* (New York: Harper and Row, 1964), 18.

4. Ralph Waldo Emerson, "The Preacher," in *The Complete Works of Ralph Waldo Emerson* (Boston: Houghton Mifflin, 1903-4).